# *A Stroke*

# *Saved My Life*

Copyright © 2020 Rose Bilal. All rights reserved. This book may not be reproduced in whole or in part without written permission from the publisher, except by a reviewer who may quote brief passages in a review; nor may any part of this book be reproduced, stored in retrieval system, or transmitted in any form or by any means, electronic, mechanical, photocopying, recording, or other, without prior written permission from the publisher.

ISBN-13:978-1-7339542-5-9 Paperback
ISBN-10:1-7339542-6-0
ISBN-13:978-1-7339542-6-6 eBook
ISBN-10:1-7339542-6-0

Library of Congress Control Number: 2020941899

Printed and bound in the United States of America
August 2020

Published by
Sula Too Publishing
Tampa, Florida
www.sulatoo.com/publishing

Tiny Book 2

# *A Stroke Saved My Life*

## *By Rose Bilal*

Tiny Book by Sula Too Publishing
A division of Sula Too LLC
Tampa Florida

*Dedicated to:*

*Robert and Penny*

top-of-mind information, that is on a loop in their heads, about those things they deem important or they are most proud. Your response to this Tiny Book may encourage an author to write a complete biography or inspire an autobiography where the rest of the story can be told.

Your story also needs to be told and now is the time. Your story is our history.

## *Preface*

Rose Bilal toured nationally and internationally with world-renowned musicians such as John Lamb, Bassist for the Duke Ellington Band, and Kenny Drew Jr., award-winning pianist. Rose has also appeared on program at Hampton House of Jazz with Trombonist/arranger, Slide Hampton.

Bilal was born in New Jersey, came of age in Philadelphia, and arrived in Tampa in 1969. Her Rhythm and Blues group appeared as opener for legends such at the O. Jays, Gladys Knight &

The Pips, Chubby Checker, The Delphonics, and Wilson Pickett.

In addition to her music career Ms. Bilal is also an actor, author, speaker, and visual artist. Her paintings and sculptures have been juried in arts festivals and galleries throughout the U.S. and can be seen in author Gary Monroe's book, "Extraordinary Interpretations." She appeared on many theater stages throughout the tri-state area including StageWorks in Tampa and American Stage in St. Petersburg. Her Theater experience has given her the confidence and ability to connect with her audience and totally engage them in her performance.

Supported by her book, "Don't Blame the Road", Rose shared her inspirational life story for women and girls throughout the country with Fran Powers' Powerstories Theater.

Now, the next chapter, in "A Stroke Saved My Life," Rose shares her moment by moment stroke experience. She reveals how it felt and what she was thinking as her world transformed and took on a life of its own. She shares how she survived "living". It is a physical and spiritual journey that is sure to move the reader to another place.

In some ways, this book is like a stroke survivor's prayer book.

# Contents

| | |
|---|---|
| Acknowledgements: | 5 |
| Preface | 8 |
| My World Stood Still | 14 |
| The Silent Killer | 23 |
| What I Awoke To | 27 |
| The Awakening | 32 |
| I Am Blessed | 46 |
| Talking To God | 53 |
| My Journey To Here | 63 |
| "Chico" | 70 |
| My Transformation | 83 |
| My Life Was Saved | 94 |
| Confirmation | 108 |
| About The Author | 121 |

## *My World Stood Still*

Believing in God has never been a question, for I have always believed in God. When we were young, my siblings and I were required to go to church. No excuses.

No excuses for us nor our parents. Even though Mom and Dad argued every day of the week; dad was always drunk on Saturday night. Regardless the failings during the week, on Sunday we were all in church.

I dutifully listened to countless Bible stories, however, they left me with more confusion and questions about God and Jesus.

I spent a large portion of my life searching for clear answers about God. I couldn't explain at the time why I needed to know who or what was God? Therefore, I went to every church in my proximity: Catholic, Baptist, Presbyterian, Seventh-day Adventists. As strange as it may sound, I even studied the Quran and practiced Islam for a few years. Surprisingly, I developed a clearer understanding of faith from Islam than from the Protestant church.

After Islam, I went for many years never giving any thought to personal spirituality. I didn't attend church. I never thought about being grateful or praying for anything. I just thought I was in control. I was enjoying my life and doing the things I wanted to do. I was happy and I thought how I was living was all there was to any - or -every - thing.

One day, a trailer for a PBS scientific program about the creation of the earth got my attention. After many years of research and testing, the scientists had found positive proof that everything on earth and beyond was created by an intelligent designer. Hearing that theory made more sense to me than the one we had been taught. We were encouraged to believe that everything began as a result of some accident.

I could never accept accidental creation for everything in nature is too perfect in the way each thing interacts with every other thing in its surroundings. For instance: It is no accident that a bird know it's supposed to fly and in a certain direction. A seed planted in dirt knows if it is to be a rose or a fruit tree.

There has to be an intelligent designer behind it all. I never gave a lot of thought to those things before. I just took it for granted that was the way things were supposed to be.

My life was all right with me! I was doing all the things I enjoyed. I was singing jazz with a jazz band. I was creating artwork, painting sculpting. I even had my artwork published in a book. Life was good.

I thought I was in control of my life. I believed all I had to do was to keep my weight under control; eat a healthy diet, get plenty of exercise and I would l be just fine. My staying on top of my health to some degree may in part be the reason I am still here for on May 9, 2013, I suffered a stroke. It was as if lightning struck and my world stopped spinning.

That day began like an ordinary day. I woke up eager to start my day. I mentally went over all the things I planned to do. After taking a shower and getting dressed, I was ready to go.

I was on the way out when Chico called me back in. At this point, I need to explain my longtime friend, Chico, was now more than a friend. We were living together. After being good friends many years, we started dating. Soon thereafter, we decided to live together. I never thought it would go any further than that. I wasn't looking for a serious relationship and I never wanted to marry. I was enjoying my life as it was; a jazz singer, visual artist and actor. I needed to be free to travel with the band or act in a play - even if the production was out of town. I didn't want the commitment that comes with marriage. Chico had been married before and it ended in divorce. He had made a vow to himself not to marry again. That was fine with me because he wouldn't be putting pressure on me to marry him.

Chico asked me to sit on the bed after calling me back into the house. I was getting irritated with him because he knew I was in a hurry. I wanted to know why he was wasting my time, instead of getting to the point. He asked me to do something I thought was more wasting of time. He asked me to raise my arms. I told him there was nothing wrong with me and that I was fine. He ignored what I said and called emergency 911.

The ambulance came, the paramedics took my vitals, put me on a stretcher and took me to ICU. I kept thinking, this is all a mistake

I'm OK. I feel fine! I was hoping I would not be held up too long in ICU so I could be released and get on with my day. I still had things to do by the end of the day.

## *The Silent Killer*

The doctor asked a lot of questions and then ordered a MRI. Chico, who had ridden in the ambulance with me, was sitting there with a worried look on his face. He thought I was going to be really upset with him for wasting my time.

When the doctor came back in, I thought he would ask Chico to leave; instead, he got the other chair in the room, came over and sat down next to me. He looked directly at me and said, "Miss Bilal, you have had a stroke. The MRI also revealed a blood clot on the right side of your brain. I must immediately perform surgery to remove it".

I sat there for a minute trying to understand how this was possible. I was not sick - I didn't even have a headache? I looked at Chico and his face told me it was really happening, no matter how good l felt.

Silence! Then the doctor said, "Miss Bilal, I need your permission right away, because we don't have any time to waste. The clot is getting ready to bleed out - if that happens you'll only have two choices - death or coma. If you go into a coma there is no guarantee you'll come out alive." This was all unbelievable to me - I was still feeling fine. I guess that's why they call it the silent killer.

I finally had to accept the fact I wouldn't be running any errands that day. I gave permission to have the surgery. It was done immediately.

Was this finally it? After all that I had survived, was this the final curtain call? I survived watching my parent's agony as their dreams literally went up in smoke with full knowledge that I was at fault.

I had survived being born in New

Jersey and growing up in the streets of Philadelphia. A person would have to talk a long time to shock me about what was in the streets. I know because I was a ring leader of a few horrible episodes. I was a female member of a male gang.

I survived prison. I survived being pregnant and hopeless. After all of this, was this the end of the road? I wrote about these life challenges in my book "Don't Blame the Road", but this is not how I wanted the story to end. I still had too much I wanted to do.

## *What I Awoke To*

I awoke in a hospital bed with Chico sitting in a chair next to me. He had been with me since we arrived at the hospital. I asked Chico to tell me everything that had happened. I had no memory of anything after being put in the ambulance. I could remember giving permission for surgery, but I didn't remember the surgery being done.

I was still not aware of what it meant to have a stroke. I had no idea of the damage done to my body. Chico explained to me that the doctor went in through the groin on my right side (femal artery) up into my brain and successfully removed the clot.

I believe the way Chico was with me caused the doctor to think he was my husband; so, he was told what was being done to me. I guess that's why he hadn't asked Chico to leave the room. After I was admitted, Chico, said to me, the only reason he was still at home and had not gone to work was he woke up thinking it was his day off. A mistake he hadn't made before.

At the time, I didn't think of what would have happened had he not been there, knew me well enough to realize something was wrong, and call 911. It had to be that Intelligent Designer controlling the way things were going. There is no other explanation for me. Only the creator knows the beginning, middle and end of everything. That's my only explanation as to why everything I needed was in place. It definitely wasn't because I was in control of what was happening. I was still in denial.

Yehovah, has a plan and purpose for everything and everybody. Only God knows what we need and when we need it. God knows everything that has to be in place for things to work like they're supposed to. Of course, at the time that wasn't a part of my thinking. When I was admitted to the hospital, I was not thinking how blessed I was to be alive. All I can remember was being angry. I was angry things were happening to me and that they were happening at that inconvenient time. I thought this was not fair to happen now. I thought all the things I had been working on were lost.

For the past month, I had been working with a booking agent in Argentina negotiating a contract for my piano player and I to do a three month gig in Dubai (It was going to pay a lot of money). I was only a few days away from signing when I ended up in hospital. I was not a happy camper.

## *The Awakening*

It was a few months later when I gave thought to how things worked out right on time. Had I not had a stroke when I did, I would have been out of the country away from Chico and all the things that had been in place to save my life. Instead of being angry, I should have been grateful.

As it turns out, having a stroke had been a good thing for me in more ways than I knew. The creator knew what I needed to slow me down and have me take a serious look at my life.

There was something else which helped me believe the Intelligent Designer was in control works from the inside or outside. I was Talking with my nurse one day and she told me the doctor who performed my surgery was one of their best doctors. He had been scheduled to be off that day - but he had decided to come in instead. I can't believe his decision was just a coincidence.

I was forced to learn to pray again. I hadn't given any thought to prayer in a long time, because I didn't see a need for it. I was doing what I needed to make life work for me. I have learned to be grateful for all the things that I previously took for granted. Now, I am grateful to be able to walk across the room; to be able to make the fingers move on my hands. I know that probably sounds trivial - I thought so too. I am aware now that everything we are able to do is because of the GRACE and MERCY of the creator.

If you ever come close to losing your life, or have to learn to walk and talk, then you'll be able to understand why I'm grateful for all the little things I once took for granted.

One day while lying in my hospital bed, I felt heat coming up from my mattress. I was afraid. I started to ring for my nurse to let her know what was happening.

Then I remembered what my mom said about prayer and the energy it produced, and thought of all my friends: jazz singers, visual artists, and actors who were praying for my recovery - this, I believe was the energy from all those prayers. The heat in the mattress was probably the healing energy being sent my way.

I was talking about God to a friend one day who said he was doubtful about God. He couldn't believe in something he couldn't see. I asked him if he believed he was breathing. He said, "of course, that's obvious ". I replied, "but you can't see the air you are breathing - I guess - you can believe in something you can't see."

I understood why my friend was disillusioned about the God he had heard about. Before I personally experienced the power of the unseen, I had doubts. In my book, "Don't Blame the Road", I wrote about all the bad things I had to overcome; such as incest, sexual abuse, teenage pregnancy, and incarceration. As bad as they all were, I deeply benefited from them all. When I think of them now, I know why I had to endure everything and the power that was at work that made them all work out. I no longer have questions about who or what God is. I know the creator was at work in my life even when I was unaware he truly existed.

Theorists believe the Intelligent Designer, loves and heals. I am a witness to that truth. There are millions of people on the earth. The Holy Spirit, Yehovah, knows their names and the needs of all of them. I am sure there are millions of people that have had something mysterious or wonderful

happen to them that they could not explain. I think it's probably because most people, like me, haven't taken the time to connect with the spirit within them - the connection to the giver of life.
Freedom

Now that I know of the power that is always at work for me, I feel I have been set free after realizing I was in prison. I was in a prison of fear and lack. I no longer have fear. I know first-hand; no matter how bad things appear, the creator is always at work to make them turn out the way they should according to HIS WILL.

The resulting events may not be the way we expected, for our initial desire may not be the best thing for us. We can't see into the future and we don't know what is best for our spirit, mind and life. Only via the creator can we overcome them.

A few years before my stroke, I was hired by the Tampa Arts Council to teach my version of paper Mache art to the teenagers incarcerated at a local juvenile facility. I saw them as young boys who had made bad decisions. I introduced myself and explained the procedure we would use to make the paper - to create the art. I told them they were free to choose anything they wanted to make.

Being young boys, I expected them to want to make cars, swords, airplanes or guns. What surprised me the most, was every one of them chose to make a cross. They made different variations on each end of the cross - but they all used the well-known shape of the cross.

When I asked them why they chose the cross as their subject, not one of them was able to say what inspired him to want to make a cross. At the time, I wasn't aware of the Master Designer, or,

I would have known what their inspiration had been. I understand how the spirit of God is always at work within us; even when we're not aware of HIS (IT'S) existence.

I hope they take time to try and find out more about themselves and discover how to make better choices. Even though they made some wrong choices, I am sure the mysterious ways of THE SPIRIT will intercede and work in their lives if they are receptive.

I thought about myself, and how being incarcerated had forced me to change the path I was following. I talked with those young men about my experience and how I'd learned to accept responsibility for my actions and reshaped them to be beneficial in my life. I told them they were smart, handsome young men and there were lots of young ladies out there looking for men like them.

I was trying to make them understand how their lives would be more productive and happy if they were free to make their own decisions and not wasting valuable time locked away in a juvenile facility.

I am free to enjoy my life and have joy in my life. Chico and I got married in 2014. I felt as though we were already married; because I was happy living with him. We had made plans to do many things together and since the State of Florida does not recognize common law marriage we thought it best to marry to avoid any legal issues that might come up.

Since I had to make use of medical assistance, Chico, needs the right to have a say in my medical care. The creator knew I would eventually have to marry - so he put the right person in my life when I needed him. He knew what I needed to change my mind about never wanting to marry. He was right again and I am grateful for what he has given me.

Every now and then I will start to feel sorry for the fact that I can't sing anymore and I will have what Chico calls a pity party. I will say a prayer and talk with Chico, because I have too many things to be grateful for to waste my time on being depressed. I wake up happy every morning realizing I've been given another day to be with family and friends and to work towards my dream, of singing again- or working on a painting or sculpture, a reality.

Life is wonderful! I won't waste

time being sad or ungrateful thinking I don't have everything I want. I'm so glad I'm free from that negative way of thinking.

## *I Am Blessed*

I have lost close friends and family members to early and unexpected deaths. I can remember wondering and hoping if they had found peace in the lives they had and if they had been happy. Some of them were younger than me. Their deaths were wake up calls for me to make the most out of every day I'm given.

There are no guarantees you'll live to see another second, minute or day. I know how easy life can slip away without you feeling a thing or being given a warning. It's a precious gift to be cherished and taken care of.

Although I still have stroke related physical aches and pains in my left hand and arm, I feel good in ways I had not considered before. I get a good feeling looking at a beautiful sunrise - not to mention the fact that I'm still here to see it. Watching the splendor of a sunrise also helps to confirm my belief in God. No power on earth can make the sun rise or set. No human being can make it rain or stop raining.

All I have to do is look around me to appreciate the power of the creator of the universe and the love he gives us every day in all things. We are given many blessings and the only thing asked of us in return is that we love God: be obedient to decrees and commandments; accept JESUS CHRIST (Yeshua Ben Josef) as our redeemer to HIM and that we love each other. I believe that's a small price to pay for the enormous treasures given to us and our family and friends.

The human body is an incredible masterpiece by the Master Designer. The Creator didn't just give us this body and then leave us alone to deal with it. He put healing mechanisms in place to keep it functioning properly and he gave us knowledge to create what we need to heal when such care is necessary.

He gave us knowledge of the technology it takes to create x-ray machines and how to perform surgery. We have been given knowledge to do amazing things with medicine, surgical, as well as, non-surgical healing. We now have knowledge of how to prevent some illnesses eliminating their ability to make us sick.

Although no matter what we do, if there's a lesson that GOD needs to teach us, or to get us to be grateful for what he gives us. If illness is the way we have to learn, then he will cause us to be ill - no matter what we do to prevent it.

God is like a father who loves his children. He teaches us what we need to learn to protect and care for the life we have been given. He doesn't want his children to have to suffer. I have experienced life long enough to finally understand the stories about God's love.

The bible was my text book from a young girl. I didn't understand the awesome power of God. That power in us and every one of his creations. The benefit to mankind and the secrets revealed by the discover of DNA is only an introduction to the miracles of God.

I wasn't thinking about God in this way, until I experienced having and surviving a stroke. It had been years since I'd been to a church.

I read countless "positive thinking" books and listened to lectures of well-known motivational speakers. I thought that was good enough for my spiritual life.

I felt no need to make a connection with the Master Planner. That didn't happen until I started praying and focusing on how things were working in my life. Thus prayers connected me to the giver of life.

## *Talking To God*

I had been in the hospital about two weeks when I began to feel like I needed to pray. It had been so long, I didn't know how to begin or what to say. The prayer I said went something like this: "Lord I know you probably don't know who I am - it's been a long time since you've heard my voice. They said in Sunday School that you are a loving and forgiving God. I hope they're right because I need your help. I'm getting worried about what's going on with me and I don't know anybody else who can give me the powerful help I need. I don't know if I'm going to be able to talk or walk again. I don't have a lot of movement on my left side - but I know you are a healer. I hope you ain't too mad at me for kicking you to the curb when things were going good for me-Amen."

I don't know if God heard my prayer, but I felt good after saying it.

A pleasant surprise arrived the next day. The pastor of Chico's church came to visit me. It surprised me because I had never met him. Although Chico, had been attending church for the past year, I never felt the need to go.

The Rev. Clovis Dunbar and his wife Lois, were the nicest people you might ever want to meet. They both took hold of my hands and prayed for my recovery. They didn't put any pressure on me to come to church, nor did they even mention the fact that I hadn't attended. I thought, well, maybe God will hear their prayer and it will give some strength to the weak words I had offered in my prayer.

Having to endure physical therapy was the worst part of having a stroke. I was wheeled down every morning to the huge gymnasium/physical therapy room. The walls were lined with a variety of exercise equipment. A car was positioned towards the end of the room, resembling those in a showroom.

Only after completing three weeks of painful exercise did I find out why the car was there. I was taken to the car, and shown how to safely get in and out of a car. As part of the therapy, I was made to get in and out of the car several times until I felt I could do it on my own.

This felt like a reward. There was no pain involved, unlike the exercises where the therapist pulled and stretched my arms and legs. I knew the exercises were necessary in order for me to regain use of the muscles I had lost, but the pain was almost unbearable.

Every so often, some of the patients brought in for therapy would be young children. It was empathetically difficult to hear their cries as they went through the exercises - unlike me, most of them were paraplegic - the muscles being forced to move on them were ones that were incapable of voluntary movement. Watching those children having to endure that kind of pain forced me to be stronger. I felt I was among the lucky ones, at least I had recent use of the muscles that no longer work and paralysis was not the cause of my not being able to use them.

I can only imagine the pain those young folks had as the therapist pulled and stretched muscles that had long since stopped functioning. I always pray for the patients having to go through that agony.

I am now a member of Refreshing Spirit Church and Ministry. I attend services every Sunday. I know my prayers are helping and there is always a need for them. When I was young and was required to go to church, I used to say to myself, "When I grow up, I'm never going to church again." I was sure that was how it was going to be, BUT GOD, knew better. As they say, "Man makes plans and God laughs." God knows what the future holds for us.

I never would have believed I would enjoy going to church every Sunday or that I'd look forward to reading the Bible or saying a prayer; to ask God for the things I need or want. I thought it was all up to me to make things happen. Sometimes I will wake up Sunday morning - especially after staying up late - feel sleepy and not want get out of bed.

I will try to justify staying in bed to sleep by saying to myself, "You don't have to go to church-you need to get your rest." I get up and going to church. Once I'm there with my church family and singing and praying with them, I'm always happy I didn't listen to that voice that told me to stay at home.

I'm getting stronger in my belief of the LIVING GOD and learning to be patient when I pray for HIS help. I have learned to do as my mother used to say, "Let go and let God."

My desires don't always work out how I want them to, but they always work out in a way that's best for me. I don't have to do anything to make things happen. All I have to do is wait on GOD and place my motion and motives as compelled by the SPIRIT. I know if it's in HIS plan, for me, He will give me what I need.

I believe the gift of being able to see into the future is not something God wanted man to have, because then in our arrogance we would see no reason to ever call his name or to thank him for his grace and mercy. I'm thankful God stopped me from travelling the road I was travelling and put me on a path of gratitude and knowledge, while I'm still alive to appreciate the gift I've been given.

I just want to tell the world of the wonderful feeling of freedom I have in knowing and understanding the power we all have at our disposal just for the asking. I am sure most people are already philosophically aware of it, however, are still tethered by sight and environment and cannot grasp the reality of SPIRIT in us and SPIRIT from YEHOVAH, THE LIVING GOD, abiding with our spirit.

## *My Journey To Here*

As I reflect on my pre-stroke life, I uncovered a pattern that give merit to the belief that there are no accidents.

My family and friends always said in order for me to get a good paying job, I had to have a good education. That worried me. I wasn't good with book learning and barely made passing grades in school. I became disillusioned with trying to learn. I convinced myself I wasn't smart, so I decided to quit school before getting a high school diploma.

After a few years of not going to school, I was feeling the need to change my thinking. I enrolled in an adult night school to get a diploma and this time around I did better. School books no longer traumatized me, I understood what I was reading. I graduated after one year with a B average. I was so proud of the G. E. D. I had earned and the fact I no longer felt too stupid to learn.

I applied for a job as an operator at the local telephone company. I was hired within a week. After working only 8 months, I was promoted to a service representative and made more money. That must have been part of the master plan for me, because I hadn't even put in for a promotion. I knew the company policy was: In order to apply for a promotion you had to have worked there for one year. I had only been there eight months, so, I wouldn't have applied for a promotion.

Sometime afterwards, I learned that my supervisor had been recommended me for the promotion. I was surprised she even knew my name and thought me worthy of a promotion. She had never spoken to me about anything and would barely mumble, "Good morning," when I came to work. I asked her why she promoted me and she said she had been paying attention to how much pride I took in my job. She further explained I was always on time and she felt I deserved the opportunity. I just thought I was in the right place at the right time. A Master Planner wasn't a part of my thoughts.

I wasn't afraid of hard work and began exploring ways to use the natural talents I had been given to make a living. I sang in the church choir and discovered my voice. When the lead singer of my friend's singing group became ill, my friend asked me to join them. I just happened to be available and did, allowing them to continue their musical tour. I sang with them for several years and made a good living. After leaving the group, I moved to Florida.

Moving to Florida, receiving my GED, working for and then leaving the telephone company, I was eager to start a new chapter in my life. I started singing jazz with the band of a saxophonist friend of mine named, Ernie Calhoun. After singing with his band for several years, I was hired to sing with a jazz combo at a jazz club on Saint Petersburg, Beach. The Master Planner was making it possible for me to earn a living without having to work a 9 to 5 corporate job.

The entertainment industry doesn't require a college degree to be a performer. It was during this time I discovered my ability to paint pictures and make sculptures with Papier Mache. I was able to sell many of my creations at art shows. This was not what I had planned for my life. I didn't have a plan. I now know the Master Planner was guiding every step I took and put me on the path that would lead me right back to the church. Learning to know God and how He is at work in my life.

I used to be ashamed to talk about God to any of my friends or family, since I did not have a relationship with the Spirit that is GOD. I thought they would think I was being a hypocrite, because I didn't attend any church and was not trying to live a good Christian life. After having what I call my awakening, I no longer care what my friends think about my relationship with the Master Planner.

# *"Chico"*

Some of the tests I was given, while in hospital, revealed I had high blood pressure and diabetes. I've been working at keeping those things under control so that I don't end up back in the hospital or worse. The day of my release from hospital the social worker responsible for discharging patients asked me, who I had to take care of me once I was at home. Chico was there with me and volunteered to be my care giver. I asked him if he was sure he wanted that responsibility? He said, "You'd do it for me wouldn't you?" I said, "I'd like to think I would."

Chico has been a great caregiver and friend. He makes my breakfast every morning before he goes to work; makes supper when he comes home; takes me shopping and looks through the racks to help me pick out the dress or outfit I want to buy; he takes me to the movies (although sometimes he grumbles at my movie choices) and to all my doctor's appointments. We go out on dates to listen to the local jazz bands. I enjoy his company. We have so much in common and know so many of the same people we always have something to talk about.

I know it sounds like I'm bragging - I am not. I'm just so grateful for the life the Master Planner has chosen for me. Chico's birth name is Albert. I have only known him as Chico - that was the name the musicians he played with called him and the one I met him as. People he grew up with or went to school with, call him as Albert.

I'm glad I wasn't in control of choosing my mate, for I had not been good at that. I always chose for all the wrong reasons. The relationship that means the most to me is the one I have with GOD. Since now that I know where everything comes from, I plan to always stay connected to the source of my happiness and the Giver of Life.

I am working on having an everlasting life or as I like to say, earn my seat in the kingdom. If there is a chance I will get to see my mother again, I would like to be able to do that. I have so many things I would like to say to her. I was never able to have the kind of relationship with Mother that I wanted. I blamed it on the fact that she was not a loving mother and I thought she didn't want the children she had. I learned later that was not the case.

I was too young to understand why my mother reacted to her children the way she did. Even though she wasn't always hugging and kissing us, I know she loved us. I wish I could let her know how sorry I am for not being able to understand what she had to endure to make her life bearable for herself.

I now know how strong a woman she had to have been, to do what she did to keep her family together and raise four children with a strong belief in God and a moral sense of right and wrong.

Even though I stayed away from

the church for many years, I still believed in the values I was raised/taught to believe. I love to read books and watch television programs that show us the beauty of the planet we live on. God's creation is absolutely amazing. The planet shows you in every way, and in everything, there is a Master Designer at work because no man can create something so magnificent from nothing.

Before having a stroke, my days were filled with so much activity I didn't think there were enough hours in a day to get everything done. My days are now filled with doing things I need to keep moving forward while recovering the things I lost due to the stroke.

I believe that too much idle time can easily lead to depression, so I make sure my days are filled and productive. I continue the exercises I learned in therapy to regain use of my left hand. I also exercise other parts of my body to keep them functioning properly and regain muscle strength. Your reading this is a sign of success. But know, I had to really focus hard to write this book. There are still things going on in my mind and body linked to the brain trauma I suffered.

Our brain controls all body functions and when there is damage to the cells it can take a long time and hard work to repair. I remember sitting on my bed when I sneezed really hard. I had sneezed like that before but, this time was different.

When I stood up and looked down, I noticed a wet spot on the bed. I wasn't pregnant, so I know my water hadn't broken. I wasn't about to give birth! I immediately called my doctor to tell him what had happened. He wasn't surprised. He calmly explained, due to the injury to my brain, I would sometimes experience my bladder emptying water without warning. He recommended I start using pull-ups in order to spare myself any future embarrassment.

I wasn't ready to hear what he was saying to me. I said, "Doc, do you remember I have a husband? I don't think I would feel very sexy around him wearing pull-ups." He said, "Would you feel sexy with a wet bottom?" So, I knew I was going to wear pull-ups.

Pull-ups are not as terrible as I imagined and my husband hasn't acted as if it makes him feel any differently about me. They can be very expensive to buy, so my health care case worker arranged to have them delivered to my home once a month free of charge (paid for by the county and the taxes I've paid).

Well, one good thing has come out of the pull-up situation. I used to worry that if I was to fall down and my dress went up I would be embarrassed by someone seeing my underwear. I no longer have to worry about that, because, if they were to see my underwear now they wouldn't be seeing my lingerie'.

Maybe, by the time they figure out what it was they saw, it would all be over and I'd be up and gone. Therefore, I would not be embarrassed. In addition, I know that Chico, would be there and would find a way to make me feel good about whatever had happened. I didn't waste too much time fretting about having to wear pull-ups.

An unplanned visit to see an old friend in St. Petersburg put life in perspective. I stopped by her home to say hello. She was not there, her husband told me she hadn't been able to work for a long time. Cancer had her fighting for her life. Cancer had done so much damage to her body she was wearing a colostomy bag.

After hearing about her dilemma, I realized my problem was insignificant. My problem was almost a blessing. I can't imagine how she felt about that. I hope she was able to realize no matter how bad it seemed - cancer had not taken her life. By the way her husband had explained her situation to me, he seemed happy to still have her with him no matter what she had to wear.

I know she will be able to work out whatever problems she has, because, she is a firm believer in the Master Designer and the power of prayer. I have a feeling she will be able to live her life as happy as she had been before cancer forced her to accept another reality.

## *My Transformation*

I spent New Year's Eve 2018 at church. I was with Chico and my church family. We brought in the New year with prayer - thanking Yehovah, for having brought us safely through the year.

I couldn't help reflecting that just a few years ago, I would have been with my band performing at some new year's gig, joining in the party celebration, not having any thought of how I made it through the year. I can't explain how good I feel knowing my life is being controlled and protected by a power greater than anything my limited understanding could imagine.

I live my post-stroke-life with happiness, security, and love. Thank you Yehovah for giving me the life you knew I needed in order to obtain the gift of the only life that truly matters - everlasting life.

Throughout my youth, I searched high and low for answers about Yehovah. However, I wasn't aware that all I had to do was pray and I would find the answers I was seeking.

Elohim, in His wisdom and mercy has given all of us a chance to receive Him in the SPIRIT that is holy. We are all created in YahWeh's image. His Holy Spirit is within us if we desire and are obedient to HIS decrees, as was with the prophets, as is today.

The connection to his power enables us to talk or pray and God will hear us. Yehovah GOD actually hears the earnest prayer of the wicked. If that were not the case, there could be no repentance or redemption in Jesus (Yeshua ) Christ (Hamashiach).

I don't have to use big, fancy words. I don't have to use correct grammar. All I have to do is speak from my heart. If it is the Will of God, all of my questions will be answered and my needs taken care of. God knows everything we need or want and HE (It "The Spirit") will deliver those. IF it is within HIS plans for you.

God is soo good. I'm still asking Him (IT" THE SPIRIT") for his help with controlling my flesh desire. Because sometimes after going through a rough experience, I will have the urge to relax by lighting up a big fat joint.

Pre-stroke, I was booked to perform monologues about the lives of several prominent historical Afro-American women who made great cultural contributions. I performed live jazz gigs at most of the local nursing homes and senior centers. I went grocery shopping for my household. I worked on a painting or a sculpture. I drove all around visiting family or friends.

Now, I have to find things I'm able to do to pass the time of day. I don't choose to watch TV all day or sit at home thinking about all the things I no longer am able to do. I choose not to buy into that recipe for depression. I choose to move forward.

I had the idea to begin going to adult senior centers and hang out with people in my age group. I did and made new friends and even found that some people, like myself, had led interesting lives. I often laughed out loud as I listened to the stories they told.

Every morning we drank coffee and had our social time together. There are so many things we can do in order to enjoy each and every day that we are given. I'm on a mission to enjoy every minute I have on this side of the grave.

Though I'm no longer able to

sing, I have a lifetime of experience. I am transforming those experiences and lessons into new ways of using my voice. Thus, in this book, I share the lessons I've learned. Maybe this is the plan that was in place for me and why I had to have the experience that caused me to lose my signing voice.

I don't question why it happened. I've learned to accept that because it happened, it was supposed to be that way. The Master Planner has not revealed to me the reason for this lesson I'm learning. I believe it is to help me build a stronger faith in the power of the Master Planner; to learn gratitude; and to learn how to pray to him for my healing and the things I need or want.

I used to fill every day of the week with plans to go everywhere I could while doing all the things I wanted; which mostly meant: hanging out with friends or family. I didn't give any thought to setting aside any time for meditation or prayer.

None of those things were important to me at the time. In fact, I didn't think they were even necessary since I believed I was the one in control of how my life worked.

Now, Even though I try to enjoy every minute of the day, I make sure to take time to say a prayer of gratitude and to read the bible. Just doing those simple things feel like I've added years to my life; because I always have more energy and I feel like I can do anything; because, I have the power of The Creator on my side.

One night, Chico and I were on the way home from a music venue in St. Petersburg, Florida. From the interstate, I looked up and saw the biggest, brightest moon I had ever seen. It was not quite a full moon, but it was so-o-o big it seemed to be following us as we drove along.

I saw it and searched my memory for a time when I would have looked at the moon and only think about the size of the moon.
Now, I think, what a glorious Master Designer, to have created something so awesomely amazing. God is great. He is all powerful. I 'm grateful HE made me aware of his presence in my life and gave my life back. I am grateful that I can be around to appreciate knowing HIM and to spread the word of HIS power and love for all HIS creation.

God is there for us from our first

breath to our last - even if we are never made aware of his existence. His love for us is greater than our lack of knowledge of him. I know he loved me enough to save my life at a time I didn't know how precious my life was to HIM; how to fully appreciate the wonderful gift I had been given by the Master Designer.

## *My Life Was Saved*

Having a stroke really did change my life. Sometimes I think it actually saved my life; because I didn't know I had high blood pressure until I was in the hospital. I am sure I would have been taken down a path to death, had I not had a stroke that put me in the position to find out about the things going on inside my body that could easily have taken my life.

God is so good to us. I am glad I discovered this while I can appreciate and depend on it to live a happy and fulfilled life.

We are now going through the Christmas holidays. I love this time of year. People seem to be more loving to each other. Total strangers will speak to me and wish me well. I wish we would stay in that frame of mind year round - but, the problems of everyday living takes over and we do not take time to be kind to each other.

Fear, jealously, racism, and all the things that divide us will take over our thinking and wipe out all the good thoughts we had for each other. Maybe we should pretend it's Christmas every day. I am sure that would make this world a better place to live.

I know that sounds corny and sentimental, but it's true. We are all created in the image of the Master Designer (spirit) and the Hosts of the Heavens (corporeal) and we have within us the ability to love, not only our family and close friends, but our neighbors as well.

We should always honor God's command, that we love one another; meaning all mankind - even those who don't look like us or share our beliefs. The more I learn about God, and His plan for me, the easier I find it to give Him the praise He deserves.

I find myself saying thank you for everything I'm able to do, no matter how small it may seem. Whenever I find something I had searched the house for - something I thought I had lost - I say: thank you God, over and over. I know His spirit led me to the spot.

The same occurs in life. God is really with us all the time, even though we can't see Him. He hears the words in our prayers and He knows what we need. I needed a stroke to help me understand how much I needed Him in my life and why I truly needed HIM. Yehovah, knew that was the way to get my undivided attention and gratitude, but, most of all he knew I need him in my life so that I could have MORE life.

Every morning after opening my eyes and realizing I've been blessed to make it through the night and wake up to another glorious sunrise; I say, thank you. I say it to myself, but I know, the Creator heard it loud and clear. I know he hears everything I say; even if I only whisper to myself. I know, because we are never alone. God is always there when we talk to him; that is the difference between flesh and spirit. His omniscient spirit is present and all encompassing. He hears everything we say and knows everything we need.

For myself, the most difficult lesson I am still learning is patience. I pray and ask God for help in getting what I need. At first I expected it to work like magic and I would instantly be given what I asked for - but, that's not how God works. I don't know what has to happen for me to get what I need or want, or if it's in God's plan for me.

I have to be patient and wait on God to give me what I need. Since I don't know what is best for me,

I ask God for my desires and then wait to see what he will bless me with. Often times, what I end up getting is much bigger and better than what I thought I needed.

I am constantly amazed at how things work out for me; it always catches me by surprise when I realize something I wanted to happen turned out another way and that way was exactly what I needed; even though I hadn't seen it that way. I think about how I never would have gotten married if it had been left entirely up to me, or, I probably would have chosen someone who probably would have let me down when I needed them most. I am so grateful that God is in charge of my life and of how to use His power to make my life everything I want it to be.

Some days when my joints are aching and I don't feel like getting out of bed, I think to myself – that it is a new day; it's a day I haven't seen before and will never see again; I'm grateful to be here to see it, in spite of the pain in my legs and arm. In fact, I'm grateful to be able to feel the pain, because, that means I still have life.

I know there are a lot of people who are no longer alive who would have chosen to be here - even in pain. I try to think of things in that way every time I find myself going down the path of regret or self-pity. I now realize how wonderful life is even when things are not going the way we think they should.

As much as I would love to sing again, I am content in the belief, that if all is God's will - I will be able to sing as I did before. If not, I know I will be able to use my voice in a way I never knew I could and have it be beneficial for my soul salvation. I know whatever the Master Designer has for me is something far greater than I could have ever imagined for myself.

Thank you God for the stroke that opened my eyes to the beautiful life I had been taking for granted. I'm grateful you took the time to align the universe with everything I needed to remind me of the journey my parents wanted their children to learn about in church; so that we would have the chance of being together again in the house of our HOLY FATHER, who loves and protects us.

While a patient in the hospital, I wasn't aware I wouldn't be able to resume the life I had before the stroke. I thought all I had to do was go home and everything would be OK. I thought I would always be able to sing because it had always been easy for me.

I was still in denial of the extent of the damage done to my mind and body; in part, because I was still feeling ok. I knew I wasn't able to use my left hand, and I was still weak on my left side - but I didn't think that had anything to do with my voice.

I have since learned that everything in the body works together, and the brain controls everything. My brain had lost a lot of the cells necessary for everything to work in harmony as before. I am still working to strengthen those cells so they can re-connect to the things they need to restore the things I've lost. I know it's going to take a long time before that will happen. I'm thankful I learned to pray and to wait on God's grace because it has kept me from being discouraged.

I know whatever God has for my life is going to be exactly what I need. Maybe even more than I could hope for. The best thing to happen to me other than still having life, is that I've learned the power of prayer and gratitude. I've even made progress in learning patience. As a patient, I had to have patience waiting on deliverance from hospital to home. I am learning to wait on God and trust I will be given exactly what I need.

Chico recently put my music sound tracks on the computer so that I can sing along with them to help make my voice stronger. I'm still not happy with the sound I hear whenever I try to sing. I have to remind myself that not only have I had a stroke, but it's been at least 5 years since I've performed.

I feel good about what I'm doing to stay positive. I just remind myself that God is in control of what happens and how fast it will happen, or most importantly, if it is supposed to happen.

## *Confirmation*

A few days ago, I was flipping through the TV channels, trying to find a good program to watch. One of the channels revealed face of an actress I admired.

She was talking about something I wanted to hear more about, I flipped back and sat down to watch the program. She was being interviewed about a book she had written. She played the lead role on "The King of Queens", one of my favorite shows and she had also been a member of Scientology, since she was a young girl. She was now exposing the hidden truth about the so-called religion of Scientology.

Some years earlier when I was searching for answers about God, I talked a friend of mine into going with me to the building where the Scientologists held their services. I wanted to know what it was about. As we left the meeting that night, neither my friend or I had a clearer understanding about God or scientology; or even if the two related in any way. I never once heard them say anything about God or Jesus the Christ. All they talked about was someone named L. Ron Hubbard.

I knew from the teachings at my church it was wrong to give praise to anyone other than God or Jesus; so, I didn't go back again. The other thing I couldn't put my finger on was; I didn't feel comfortable being there. I felt as if we were being watched by everyone.

When we asked to use the rest room, we weren't allowed to go alone, we had to be escorted by a few of the members who waited outside, so they could escort us back to our seats. It was as if they were afraid we would see something we weren't supposed to.

After I heard the interview by the

former member, I understood why we were followed. I'm thankful I had learned earlier, there's nothing hidden about God and the message He has is free for us all. I felt I wasn't at a place where I would get the spiritual guidance I was searching for knowing now God had other plans for my life.

It seems every experience I've had led me in the direction I was to go in. I believe that to be true because I was always in the place I needed to be in for things to work out in my favor; even though at one time in my life I was in an abusive relationship - it ended up being the place I needed to be to initiate the singing career I was able to enjoy years later.

My boyfriend/abuser was the leader of the singing group I joined. It was through my relationship with him, I worked with a singing group and world renown entertainers; travel the globe and make lots of money.

The only thing I thought I was missing was love. I had no idea at the time I was on a path that would lead me to the two greatest loves of my life. I am talking about my husband and the Master Designer, Yehovah God.

When I think back to how I lived

my life before the stroke, I sometimes feel as if I am now living a new life.

Back when I believed I was in control of my life, I gave no thought to how magnificent the human body is or to the Master Designer that created it. Coming close to death has been to me like coming out of a dark tunnel into daylight. I see things in a way I never saw them before.

I wonder, if I'm experiencing what my mother referred to as being born again? Maybe that's what is meant by having a new life after all. Having a renewed mind. I do have a new way of walking; a new way of talking; and a new way of thinking. I'm not the same as I used to be. I know that GOD, YHWH, is in control of my life.

I no longer have to live in the dark - all I have to do is walk in the light - the light that is provided for me by my HOLY FATHER who loves me. Although my health is not what I'd like it to be, I feel better than I've ever felt before.

I wish my mother was still alive to see how I voluntarily go to church on Sundays. I know it would make her soul happy to know her struggle for her children to know God was not a total loss. I'm grateful that God gave me parents who, in spite of their faults, knew the reason for their existence, and the responsibility they had to pass it on to their children.

I was being blessed by God long before I was aware of His presence in my life. Whenever I see children being abused or neglected by their parents, I would say to myself, it's too bad those children couldn't pick the parents they wanted before they were born; because I didn't think those parents deserved to have children.

I probably wouldn't have picked

the parents I had and my judgement would have been wrong - again. I know why God says only He is capable of judgement, benign or malignant, because only HE, Yehovah, knows what is in our hearts, or what is in His plan for us.

Before I had a stroke I was doing a gig at the Columbia Cafe in Channelside, in downtown Tampa. I worked every Saturday from 6 p.m. to 9 p.m. The Columbia Cafe is situated along the Hillsborough River. I used a keyboard as a prop to simulate a piano and I sang using piano tracks recorded by my good friend, pianist, Kevin

E. Wilder.

I worked with another musician and friend, drummer, Billy Mays. Billy was 90 years young and was still able to transport his drums to and from the gig, as well as keep a fantastic beat to the music I sang. I loved working at the Columbia Cafe. We played out on the mezzanine where we watched row boats go by, and giant cruise ships that would dock next door to the Cafe.

Sometimes the passengers on the ship would stand on deck and listen to the songs Billy and I played. They would applaud loudly for their favorite songs. Billy and I, enjoyed playing for the customers eating at the cafe and for the people passing by. We both just loved the music and playing there together.

Music is so much a connector of spirits and less a stimulus for dance. As much as I thank Jehovah for music, I thank that SPIRIT for a stroke that connected me to my soul and I am a complete person for it.

My hope today is that my loved ones and close friends, of whom I love as well, do not have to be brought into awareness of a total self, flesh and spirit, by a catastrophic event in their lives; but that those still unaware, will receive the awakening of all of their existence as being ONE.

## *About The Author*

*Rose Bilal and Al "Chico" Arenas*

Until her stroke, Rose Bilal lived a life of crime, fame and fortune. From the streets of New Jersey and Philadelphia to the big stage as a sought after performer. Her story is told in a page turner memoir, "Don't Blame The Road". She lived a fast and extraordinary life and in some ways, too fast.

In "A Stroke Saved My Life" Rose details how the stroke she suffered in 2013, altered everything, even her soul.

# RESOURCES

Go to <u>veromundo.store/resources-arthur/</u> or use the QR Code provided to access a list of short videos, documentaries, and articles available online about Arthur and Mikael.

**EL REY ARTHUR AudioBook**
MP3 Downloadable is available at
www.veromundo.store